Arson & Prophets

Poems by

Scott Withiam

The Ashland Poetry Press
Ashland University
Ashland, Ohio 44805

Acknowledgment is made to the following magazines in which these poems first appeared:

The Adirondack Review: "Fate"
Blue Mesa Review: "The Widow's Drought Dream"
Cimarron Review: "The Rain Falling, Falling Short of Falling on Me"
Cream City Review: "Beautiful Baby"
Drunken Boat: "Sea Roses"
Farmer's Market: "Frog in a Boat"
Field: "Culture," "Spared"
Fine Madness: "Cows, in Their Quiet Way"
The Florida Review: "Postcard"
Green Mountains Review: "Pleasure," "Nobody's Who They Were,"
    "Morning Is Best"
The Greensboro Review: "The Baby Shower"
Harvard Review: "Two Old Horses," "Therapy"
Icarus: "Bad Machine"
Inkwell Magazine: "Tired of Raking"
The Laurel Review: "My Double Comes Home," "Bundle"
The MacGuffin: "Apology to the Packed Deli"
The Madison Review: "Provisions"
Marlboro Review: "History Abroad"
The Massachusetts Review: "Reunion Break"
Nightsun: "Love Poem with Balls"
Paragraph: "The Blue Purse"
Pleiades: "Hollow Points"
Ploughshares: "The Days of Blue," "Winter Apples," "Walk Right
    In," "Assimilation"
Poet Lore: "Nocturne"
Press: "Cloak of Beef"
Rhino: "Bliss"
River Styx: "The House That Goldilocks Built"
The Sandhills Review: "Hungry Nation"
    (appeared in a different form and previously titled "Ruth")
The Sow's Ear Poetry Review: "The Green Suit"
The Sun: "Talking to Trees"
Sycamore Review: "At 18 or 19"
Third Coast: "Proportions," "Monster Desire"
Two Rivers Review: "Considering Age and Memory Loss,
    Remembering My First Boat"

Printed in the United States of America

ISBN: 0-912-592-52-4

Library of Congress Catalog Card Number: 2003093939

Cover design: Catherine Kirby

Cover drawing: Gretchen Troibner

For my wife, Pam,
and my mother, Jean,
and in memory of my father, Paul

Contents

III. Compensatorium

I. Nobody's Who They Were

Hollow Points

In my youth, the job of stripping lint from the bottom
of the Laundromat's dryers; the fun part—sorting out
the safety pins; small coins, brightened, still hot;
.22 hollow points, which, considering the heat
and banging, should have gone off,

but didn't. Oh the tendency, going over things gone through,
looking back—someone's tough life, bitter life, didn't come out right
life. My life, your life. Mostly receipts, reminders,
matchbooks macerated into hard little pills. Today I found one
owl pellet, the remains of a cardinal

from which everything had been extracted,
savored. What more can we ask?
The bones and bright feathers compacted
into a nice little package, and handed back
for someone else to discover again. Very neat; very clean.

Monster Desire

Plaque of moss burning
bright green—wooden green smile,
green teeth, monstrous, what one gets
failing to brush with fire growing with every douse of spring rain,
somehow, somewhat like what happens
when one takes old prescribed medication that's been lying around,
centrally, minorly thinking, *Uh-oh, oh God, I'm getting it back again—*
a cold,
a sore throat,
and now, and now,

never getting something back again.
Never,
the worst reaction, the flush rash on your teeth, my itchy teeth,
what the earth is—never getting something back again,
what the earth screams every page of rain laid down

and blowing left to right.
How should you read this? Well, my friend,
I speed read with the robins.
Besides being our cheery spring eternal lies,
that is what robins can really do—
speed read desire off the page,
why they never turn their head,
a little hop, a little hop and really

feel for the worm.
Quite a feat with the feet, feeling
for that worm, that worm working at our feet. It all comes down
to the worm, but it's nothing, none of it, nothing
till impaled,
held,
held up,
held
till motionless.
What do you mean you don't want it?

Nobody's Who They Were

Sprinting out of the creek and across his backyard, water dripping through his cupped hands, beaming, beaming, the boy's got a hold of something, something beautiful to share, the tiniest baby crayfish ever, watery body and limbs so transparent,

but all the water's gone by the time he reaches his front door. The creature's acrobatic flips stop; it drags its shrinking self across the boy's palm, tickling like a dry watercolor brush toward the edge. The boy laughs a little nervous laugh by himself, then runs the crayfish inside, inside for

help. It's Memorial Day. A bunch of parade-ready men drinking coffee and beer watch grandmother help grandfather into his uniform. "It's too damn small. I'm not going to wear it," grandfather snorts. "Oh come on, suck it up," says grandmother, "nobody's who they were."

There's one soldier in the living room not so busy with laughter. Face pressed against the picture window, he's fixed on the creek, some part of him down there. *Nobody's who they were?* The panicked boy holds the crayfish out to him. The soldier plucks it from the boy's palm, plops it into his coffee and finishes both off.

That's it! That does it! I stomp down to the creek, fish under a rock and pull out the soldier who gulped the crayfish. With him floating in my leaking hands say, "That was the smallest thing I ever saw." It's never that clear. He's dragging himself across my palm, a miniature man shot in both legs, screaming for mercy.

He saved the crayfish from blind cruelty; he couldn't stand to see it happen again. He did good, the right thing, as is always the desire, the impulse. And I swallowed him.

Nocturne

I woke as her piano, both her hands—one following the other—in a run along my thigh, down my stomach, what was Debussy or Chopin, unless I moved. I was overwhelmed by how what she did in the day ran seamlessly into the night and back again. I feared her preparation, not the depth of memory, but the room for it. My days broke differently. I went from a stupid job to a five o'clock habit. They carried me needful into different bars and apartments like hers. That morning in her house, my body rang, a round ringing I never felt before, sustained like a door to the heart, or the way the heart circles a feeling. I watched her at total rest and felt I could love her, because I couldn't. As soon as she woke, she promised someday to bring me with her downtown to the great Steinway rooms, which sounded dark and cavernous, yet held some fleeting possibility for me to be there with her in her music while she played some other night. There, she said, one after another I could open their tops and see how differently each one sang back—something I already knew. I fell off again, and then woke to a tic-tic-tic in the practice room, her singing her etudes without touching a key. She kept messing with the metronome, trying to get the tempo right, locking the weight into the measured settings on the arm.

Walk Right In

All summer and fall the couple floats hand in hand from work at the sheltered workshop. Hand in hand in their second hand sleeveless oxford shirts. With target tattoos on their deltoids. Even in the winter, the same way, hand in hand, although bundled up in second hand wool coats. One snowy evening, right after they pass by like this, Jack, a regular at the bar which nightly watches the couple, says that he's heard they claim to hold hands even when they sleep, and this way stay aware of the other's dreams. "They can even enter each other's dreams if they wish," Jack says. They *are* nuts. Bizarre; ridiculous claim. And for what purpose—true or not—would one enter a dream? That's the kind of conversation that ripples the bar till the barmaid, Louise, says, "Because they could change it. They could walk right in on any dream gone sour and turn it around." And that puts an end to the debate with a total hush. Except one bitter night about a week later the couple walks right in, pulls up chairs in the lounge and sits holding hands beneath one of the barely used, cozy round tables. His rotten and her chipped teeth chatter. They refuse any offers to drink to get warm. The longer they sit, the place turns creepy, somber. Realizing this isn't good for anyone's business, Frank, the bartender, finally shouts, "Then, what the hell do you want?" "Okay, come on," his partner says, hauling him up by his coat sleeve, tugging him toward the door, "it's time to get home." She pushes him out, and in the entrance turns around to address the bar. "Thanks for letting us get warm for a minute. We didn't mean to bother. Sorry, too, about Mike. He does a good job at work." Her thick, out-of-date glasses make her eyes wide as dolls', and because, after she speaks, the whole bar almost falls in, they think, *She's warming up, getting ready, once Mike's asleep, to go in, straight up his arm and into his head so to set things right.* Right after they're gone, Frank buys a round of drinks, and Jack, who claims he knows all about them, starts up with, "I hear Mike takes advantage of her." *Wouldn't any one of us here?* the bar thinks. And before another debate stirs and ends there, it's silent.

Talking to Trees

A doctor, so angry at the inconvenience of being called in to suture a suicidal prisoner's wrists, said, "I'll make sure he doesn't do that again," and sewed him up without an anesthetic. That doctor was employed by the state to cut medical costs. He still is. No one knew that my wife lost her job for taking her protest to the top, for blowing the whistle, that she set out for an early-morning run the next day to leave it all behind, to start fresh, especially not the mother raccoon at the roadside standing on her haunches as my wife chugged by. Not aggressive, not in defense, but more, standing over her unmoving baby. Only when times are desperate do appearances like this occur. They stared at each other for a few seconds, and then the coon turned and sauntered off. The baby's belly moved. My wife peeled off an outer layer, the new, long-sleeved cotton T-shirt that all the way around said SAUCONY, and wrapped the baby in it. And she spoke to the dark white-pine row where she sensed the mother watched. "I'll do what I can." And then she ran, all the way watching the baby, its closed eyes inside the fur rings ringed again with wet, as were the mouth, the nose, all signs of living rolled with dirt. Home, she grabbed the cordless phone off the kitchen wall, shut herself in the downstairs bathroom, put down the toilet seat, and sat with the baby coon between her feet. The animal-control officer, local vets, wildlife agencies, state agencies—those who answered—said, "Rabies." *Rabies.* Consumed with fear of the disease, she thought. Their hesitation to care is itself consumptive. "Kill it, cut off its head and turn it in for state testing," they said. The last response like that, she snapped, "It's a fucking baby raccoon for Christ's sake." Immediately placed on hold, she stood, saw herself in the vanity mirror, and asked, "What good is it?" Which is when another person on the other end spoke: "What you've described sounds like internal injuries. The animal will be euthanized anyway. Bring it in as soon as possible," he said, as if all mankind depended on it, meaning, she knew, the same as the others before, only measured, more official, conscious. Worse. As if all of mankind depended on it, she took the baby back. Its body breathing unevenly at her feet, she faced the pines and began calling, coaxing the disappeared mother back. Which is when the first car sped by, one of many neighbor commuters who later made a point of telling me, "I saw your wife talking to trees." To which I said, "Absolutely. Don't you?"

8

Provisions

When something washes up in our seaside community,
we never ask, "Whose is it?"
It's automatically ours,
exactly what we need.

A small, round cast-iron pedestal table sits there
this morning, out on the fingertip of sand
extending from the shocking green salt marsh.

And thrown to the table's top
as if the bar has closed for the day to clean up
is a wooden ladder-back chair,
telescoped legs, shot cane seat.
The ocean slowly backs away, admires its arrangement.

One of us is already out there hauling back the table.
He doesn't realize how heavy it is.
The table over his head, this thought presses him:
  An ocean wants to sit still, to admire less than be admired.

He quickly drops that and goes for the chair.
Rather than pick it up, sits in it. Doesn't fall through,
but sinks till the legs disappear. His ass is all wet.

He has company. Next to him
a broken hull, a flipped,
horseshoe crab shell, the insides picked clean.
What else to call these but pieces of dreams?

Now the fiddler crabs approach,
sideways, as if from behind the same stage,
en masse, hundreds, maybe thousands
making a low whisper in the eel grass.
And lift the man up. There are provisions here
to get carried away. Thank God.
That's how those of us who traveled here to live have lasted.

Cows, in Their Quiet Way

Salt licks in red, white, and blue laid out before them,
but they don't care. Whatever

color in their path—bawling along,
flies in pursuit—they idly slosh and slap the blocks all day.

Tonight, they're high upon the hill, folded there
under the stars, expectant, awaiting a good thing's

squirt out of the sky. A miracle
would be for them to take more initiative,

kick up their arses and return directly to the farmer,
demand to choose the salt block colors,

then even tongue sculpt the blocks into something
recognizable, of worth. What? Skittish deer

stand at the edge of the field shivering.
They're going to shatter. What's *their* problem?

The salt blocks. The licks aren't right.
There go the deer. They're always going off.

There's always something wrong. Okay, I see. Day
to day the cows strip down the blocks

to leave the deer little to fret over.

Assimilation

Already at work—squatting, preening—
the Cambodians weed the cranberry bog.
They're close to the earth like mourning doves

foraging below the bird feeder—the last to come,
to take what others dropped. There's no moaning.
They're chatty, a giddy cackle carries among them

while they move together. They're alive as the frogs
that ga-dung in the ditches. Faint yellow clouds
of pine and oak pollen slip down, coat them.

The expert on their boombox calls it a natural response.
To what, it's not clear. Every bright surface dimmed,
subtly altered. The crew boss swings by

in a new midnight blue van. He's traded in
his wide-brimmed straw hat for a baseball cap.
He oversees. He squints at his own kind.

Cloak of Beef

Naked from the waist up,
the model dons a fresh side of beef.
What to call it? A cape of flesh,
a burden? It does make one sure-footed,
and yet simultaneously gives
the appearance of someone
inching toward an ocean cliff
strapped to a hang glider. Have to
like those options. The blood
streaked down the model's back
and stomach—dried like rouge
on the face at someone's funeral.
Why does anyone—dead or alive—
wear make-up to a funeral?
Well, say this about it, it's easier to take off
than put on. And the model
struggles, breathes
so hard it's as if he's trying to blow
life back into the thing,
or maybe even live in it—
the highest aspiration of all our robes.
This is a brutal country,
everything open, exposed.
The muscles in his back, those
tubes running up either side of the spine,
they're so pronounced that
no one argues that they're not pleased
to be alive, so reminiscent of bulls
made to dance again in fire light,
those paintings on the cave walls
of Lascaux. But who can take shelter in that?

Reunion Break

Inside the gym, when the dance began, I didn't want to admit
    something. My
Age or era, I thought. That's when an ancient Greek Father faded in
    on my left

And asked me to step outside. Not to fight. To think.
Once out in the parking lot, he stared at the throbbing brick
    gymnasium.

"A glimpse of the future I never would have imagined," he said.
Maybe that's my problem, I thought. *I expected more*

At this juncture. "It's too hot. We need air," someone inside
    hollered.
The fire door kicked open.

He looked perplexed.
Out poured some dancers. They continued gyrating

In the gel-colored pads of DJ lights that wandered about.
"There's no fire," he said, "just lights that only reach so far,

Fly by or go right through." Sprawled on my car's hood,
Distantly fixed on the dance, I understood what he said

As exactly what I really didn't want to admit.
"To come this far," I said, "and life so, so . . . ."

"So dangerously shaped," said the Greek, stroking my Honda's nose.
"Would you take me for a ride?" "Sure," I said, "hop in,"

But thought, *How to get myself out of this?*
Think. I started the engine and flipped on the head lights.

In them my wife now spun, draped in a glittering, sheer cloth
One nostalgic classmate brought. "Moth," marveled the Greek,

"Beautiful moth into the flame." "I'm going to stay and dance with her," I said. "You take the car out yourself, see what it does."

"Are you for real?" he asked.
"It's all yours," I said, and he took it.

The Baby Shower

It's quite possible I was born
the day I decided to tell a big truth,
determined to cleanse my soul,
go clean slate, and sat—not quite like this—expecting, maybe,
the hoopla and balloons—
awaiting the rewards for bravery.
And got my ass spanked good.

And though breathing disappointment,
I kept right on pushing, telling the truth,
each time expecting only good results, like the time
I told my friend her fiancee was intolerable.
I couldn't see the lines I was drawing in the sand,
the either / or truth creates.
Didn't see it till today

when the pregnant mother waddled her way in,
and standing before her, some phony
moved his hands in the air as if sculpting,
as if moving his hands over the contour of her belly,
saying, "What is it about that shape? Perfect, I just love that shape."
As an apology for all my earlier mistakes,
I simply chimed in, *"Yes, a shape so close to the earth,*

earthy." And the mother looked at me as if she'd just given birth
and it wasn't her baby, the look saying, This can't be you.
Is this really you, the guy I know
not out on his own, not telling the truth?
And so I tried:
"You're . . . you're a tear drop. You're a Hershey Kiss."
The mother scowled over the insinuated weight.

And then came truth herself,
a woman who introduced herself as Jane,
because, as she said, though I'd met her a number of times before
I never remember her because she's always

changing her hair style, the color.
"Have you met my husband, Bill?" she asked. "He's a funeral director."
Bill changed jobs mid-career,

was once an air traffic controller.
He's still in the Reserves, in minutes can set up a landing strip
in any football-sized field. On one hand,
I didn't give a shit. But there were the huge bodies
of all those to whom I'd told the truth
landing without a glitch, no accidents.
On the other hand, I wanted his know-how.

Postcard

Loving every minute . . .
Now that I write it—impossible.
Don't get me wrong, everything—
the cabin, natives, food, view—
especially that—were . . . . Right
now a white egret dines at low tide—
that tipped mirror—a school of fry
locked in a tidal pool.
It's so all around cruel.
The cursed bird stabs and stabs
and is nowhere—yet—all its movements
so connected to the head.

Making This Nation a Better Place to Live

This morning I'll try and write a speech to sway millions into action, though what that action might be I don't know. The hemlocks that surround me are still, except when the little bit of water that collects builds weight on a branch, then falls through to the next branch, caused by the fourth straight day of drizzle, the drizzle producing a faint, metallic ting on the lake. Something transporting in that ting. The light, too, enough light to match a tight basement function hall I once knew, enough light again to grow a little grass on each step down, that grass still expertly maintained by human travel. The ting coming from inside that hall—the tinkling of silverware on glass—and quickly builds to banging and the chant, "Come out, Come out." The crowd, familiar now, as is all they want. Dessert served and devoured, their desire is to get up and dance. But first, they need to thank the woman who, once again, made this feast possible, who derives so much joy from making them full and happy. There she is: Ruth. The only face I really remember. What can she say? A quick wave to the cheer, grab a picked over garnish tray—a few loose radishes and black olives rolling—and hustle back into the kitchen. A kitchen over fussed with foil and turkey cavities boiling in pots. Leftovers and prep. Already focused on the next gathering. The next branch. I was a boy then and there was something I knew, but felt too small to say. And now the hemlocks shake themselves out with a breeze. Ruth wanted to dance. When she stood there in front of everyone, I wanted to sneak up behind her, untie the little knot behind her neck, slip the apron loop over her head, allow her white bib to drop to her waist, so that everyone saw the blue satin dress underneath. What would that do? The dress would make water of the light; someone might notice how like water her necklace beads grew larger the deeper they stretched. And somewhere some wood scraping would not be the unloaded branches of pleased trees, but a man pushing back his chair, rising to ask Ruth to the dance floor.

Proportions

When my sister said she was leaving me for the Church,
I felt cheated. I hate God, I told her.
That's one monstrous feeling, she said.
And as she walked away for good, all I could do was think

She's right. In comparison,
this country, its wacky preoccupations,
seems a mouse scurrying
beneath my feet. The world,
a dark basement. Damp.
Growing smaller. The days go by

and I rarely think about what I said,
more how the moment I said it
my body shuddered
like an old boiler firing,
wrestling with itself to come on.

Then today, the story by a friend in maintenance,
himself in the basement of an unfamiliar building,
and spooked by the firing—
the same kind of boiler.
Only he lurched back,
and by freak accident
crushed a mouse scurrying behind him.

Under the heel of his work boot, he said,
he never felt a thing till he looked down.
And what did I think? That this country is dead,
the world flat and ready to be picked up by the tail and tossed
    in the can?

No, I saw the mouse for what it was—
a frail thing, a pliant being,
that forces itself into tight,
impossible places.

Winter Apple

The last withered one
held so long
by such a weak tree.
Who needed who?
I'll never know. It's over.
The apple just dropped to the snow crust.
It's the only color in the field.
The one-eyed gray squirrel finds it
by positioning his head to see the side blind to him.
I could be talking about any of those absolutes
that one is tempted to capitalize
and live under. Like an angel,
the squirrel walks the crust without falling through.
Now he's trying to hog the apple for himself.
Too big for his mouth, he overruns it.
Right behind him, a crow swoops down
and whoops, it wasn't what he thought.
Embarrassed, he looks around to see if anyone saw him,
then *out of here*. Absolutes, rarely in the flesh.
More birds, more squirrels
come to take their whack at it,
and each whack takes it further from the tree.

II. The Days of Blue

Fate

We moved in the height of summer, and halfway down every hill the borrowed truck overheated. Our first day at Goodyear Lake my family was five days late. Someone else was moving into our cottage. Jane, the landlady, had another cottage open—next to hers on the other side of the lake. "What can we do?" my mother said. "Take it," my father said. That straightened out, my new playmate, Jane's girl, Kate, took me home to the other side. Instead of a direct course, Kate cut a long loop, sharply wrenching the boat back and forth the whole way. The water skimmed my knuckles glued to the gunwales, and forced out of the water the engine moaned. Jane—having already reached home by car—stood on shore dressed in nothing but a slip, and frantically waved us in. Once we struck land, Ralph, Kate's dog, jumped out of the boat and barfed. I bent over, claimed a small stone and kissed it. "Good dog," Kate said. "What were you thinking? What came over you?" Jane screamed. "What?" Kate said. "What did I do? I didn't do anything." "That's it!" Jane said, handing me the slip, heading for Goodyear's bath-warm water. There wasn't time to turn around. A painter pulled up in a big truck with a tank and compressor on the back. The cottage windows already masked off, he spray-gunned the rest of our cottage white. Soon, it began to snow. Worse, that's all the television gave—a snowy picture and an even static. The cottage was full of holes and freezing. The parents argued, my mother saying the experiment was a bust, and she wanted to move; my father replying, "What are you doing thinking it's no good when there's no place else to go?" And then he stormed out of our one white door, a door no one else could find but us. Just up the street lived a long time resident named Sally. She always had company and was always ready with mixed drinks the color of antifreeze, something we could have used right from the start, my father said. Sally kept a mimicking tropical bird which had been around Goodyear for as long as she had. It talked a lot of nonsense. Sally had two house rules: Sit here and listen; it's free.

Bad Machine

Words spoken just kept going till falling into orbits like satellites, and this machine—whatever it looked like, however it worked—had only to track them down, tune them in. My father made that up to make me stop, consider more carefully what I was going to say before I said it. There never was such a machine, though I never bothered to check. At 15, I was too interested in argument, in this case, proving that hunger magnified hearing. Who needed machines? We needed only to believe in human capability. Take Cesar Chavez, I said, fasting two weeks to make the world listen, standing in the middle of a pre-trial hearing and out of the blue saying, "There's been a terrible accident." No one else heard the crash. No one believed till sirens suddenly converged. Sirens sang. Proof, see? And that's what I remember. Nothing of politics or history, only that I won, smashed that machine. But what I hear is how, in the end, my father hungered for forgiveness of his absences. And, how I was too careful about what I should say. What about right now? I just redistributed a load of wash so it wouldn't thump-thump. And in order to get the kids back to sleep, carried each one into the laundry room. Altogether slapping the machine, making it *boom,* saying, "Bad machine, bad machine." "Speak to it," they said. "Kiss it goodnight."

Therapy

"I just get all the lights out," I'm telling my therapist, "pop open a beer and turn on the ball game when the knocking starts at my front door. *Let me in. I've been stabbed.* So, I yell back at him through the door, 'What do you expect? You walk around all night in one of the darkest, most dangerous parts of town.'" That's why it's so hard to help him—he's just like you," my therapist says. "It's okay, go ahead. You can open the door now." So I do. Buckled over, the guy stumbles across the Persian rug and flops down on my empty couch. He tears open his Hawaiian shirt to show us his gut, the tiny, blackened hole. "Puncture wound," I say, "normally not something to fool around with, you can't tell how serious they are. But in this case— I've seen this so many times before—I can tell you, it's a scratch." *A fucking screwdriver,* the guy groans. "Phillips head or regular?" my therapist asks. "Jesus, that's awful. Where are you going with this?" I ask my therapist. "Did your father ever show you the difference?"

Pleasure

One day in the park, a thin, three-legged stray dog came to Richard's side. Richard named him, Duke. Like Duke, Richard couldn't touch himself without falling over, and consequently, he always met with a lack of success in life, especially in the mating game, which concerned him—next to himself—the most. But God is good. Richard quickly discovered that wherever Duke followed, people, women especially, fell all over him. And so, he took Duke home and fed him better than himself. What is it about three-legged dogs and women? I'll tell you, but you already know—sympathy, that a man visibly exhibits so much care for a poor thing like himself. But sympathy, too, has a phantom leg, which was Richard's impersonation of the caring soul, while he cared nothing for the blindly devoted Duke. And that is one famished leg to feed. Richard was its food. So he was fattened. With a daily healthier, shinier Duke at his side, to Richard came the most beautiful women, and every delight of the body those women might offer, sometimes the trickling of scented oils, strategically placed grapes, or buttons of chocolate fixed with dabs of honey to be . . . . Let your imagination travel, it's all true, it all happened, except that every one of these occasions lead—maybe for you, also—to the most tantalizing question: "Tell me, how did it happen?" the women asked. "How did Duke lose the leg?" This always at the peak sexual moment, and never an ending. Because Richard had no answer. He never cared enough about Duke to ask. If he had, Duke would have told him: "I was born like this."

Culture

Thirty years too late the restaurant begins to pulse red for old girl-friend, Peg, and me, so I quickly slide out of our window booth, push through a beaded curtain into the kitchen where, at the island table, a Chinese family feverishly throws itself together. "Is something wrong?" the oldest asks. "MSG?" I venture. "Never heard of him," sings the whole chorus dressed in white aprons. Why, then, do I struggle for oxygen and stumble through a tight pantry, stepping over—sometimes into—cardboard boxes to escape out the back door? Peg in curious pursuit, we burst into the still summer night, and standing in the corner of the alley a dwarf weeping cherry dips its blossomed sprays into a four foot plastic pool. "Culture," she says, while I kick a waxy lettuce box off of my foot, "what we keep alive." "For sure," I say, "and how. Come here." Over the pool arches an ornate footbridge, so tiny, so steep that when I kiss her upon it we're skyscrapers waving in high winds, buildings kissing, glass splinters raining down. Something nibbles wherever we sprinkle over the surface of the pool.

Bliss

She snatched the snapping turtle up with her bare hands as it crossed the yard near the roses, pulled it to her chest and rubbed noses. "Ow, I will call you James," she said. "James Brown, because now you live in my cardboard box." He scratched the walls incessantly, and barely supported himself on his hind stumps. *Scriiitch, ka-thump; scriiitch, ka-thump.* "The sound of happiness," she said. "When you're happy, I'm happy, too." She'd been around just long enough to know how to play it down. Officially, he was her agent. She introduced him to the press this way when strolling in public, sometimes calling him "My secret agent, James, James Bond," winking, and leaving a trail of giggles and photographers. Soon, though, she granted one interview. "If James Beard taught me anything about success, it's to put my head in the box right down here with him, pass on the lettuce, and go for the meat," she said, then nibbled gently behind the place where there should have been ears, he, in kind, returning the gesture.

History Abroad

This country has vast, columned historical museums which take up more than three-fourths of the livable space. No one enters them. They sit outside and stare into the ivy that climbs the brick walls. How do countrymen discern who they are, how they arrived where they're at? I'm seated at one of a thousand outdoor cafés where they eat. The ivy's filled with sparrows and their chatter. The blowing newspapers worry about a fourth aimless generation. There's a little boy pulling like mad on his straw, trying to savor what's left on the bottom. Instead of admonishing him for being rude or to leave a little behind, his mother says, "That sounds like liposuction. That's good, Jacky. Get rid of all of it." *The same way they treat history*. A man sitting alone two tables away chews something large and difficult. Whatever it is, he's stuffing that into his straw. He blows it right in front of my face. "I want her the way she was," he says. "Me, too," I shout. That little boy is out of his seat and pointing at one of the café trees wrapped in little white lights which define it. He's screaming that there's a tiny woman in exercise tights stuck headfirst into the tree; she has no behind. "That's how she wanted it," the man says, and stomps off.

The Blue Purse

Dim lit and isolated the far end of the airport terminal where she dropped her bags, looked heavenward at the ceiling and screamed, "This is the fifth transfixed, tan-uniformed jerk I've been sent to." Then, to the slumped, thin man in the glass booth: "My navy blue leather purse, you people better not have lost it goddamn it. Do you know how much it cost? Do you?" The thin man speaking another language spun off of his stool and easily slipped out of the booth door, disappeared. "Finally," she said, "I'm getting somewhere." Shortly, a loud pop of electricity, the sound of creaking wheels, the whole wall before her eyes folding back. "What a country," she said. Behind the wall? Nothing but a huge, unlit open space like an empty warehouse or a vacated department store. At the far end, where it was totally black, a flashlight came on, bobbed towards her till she could make out who was behind it—the same skinny man in the booth. With a wave of the flashlight, he gestured for her to follow him. Into the dark and down a supermarket length aisle of high, industrial-sized metal shelves stacked with unclaimed luggage he took her searching. *What am I thinking?* she thought, *What if . . . ?* It's then he stopped, as if reading her mind, turned around, grinned, nodded for her to turn around. His flashlight beam fixed on a strapped Styrofoam box, OJOS printed in big letters on the side. Also, stamped all over the box: LIVE ORGANS. DO NOT LEAVE UNATTENDED. LIVE ORGANS. DO NOT LEAVE UNATTENDED. There! There was her blue purse. "Mine," she screamed, jumped up and snatched the purse, ran with it for the open wall, for the dim light and faint hum of the terminal. The purse was fine, not a thing inside it disturbed. Nothing. Amazing.

Bluebirds (with Floss)

Then we have a world of things to do, so long as there is light,
in fact we hardly have time to look at one another a bit.
    —Henri Michaux, "I Am Writing to You From a Far-Off Country"

Here I am in the bathroom mirror craning, stretching, my mouth wide open. The floss just frayed, bunched between two capped lower molars, then broke off. There isn't enough time to do anything with it. It's *hurry up, get downstairs,* where, rounding up the last of her CHEERIOS floating loose in the bowl, and our kids, already late for work—*something so small magnifies in the mouth*—my wife tries to bring me up-to-date or up-to-speed. "I miss you. Yesterday," she says, "did I tell you? Last night I rescued a baby bird, a sparrow. Please get out of that mirror. Did you hear me, Jennifer? Your brother needs some time in there, too. After work, getting out of my car, I heard its troubled *cheep, cheep, cheep.*" "I was right here. Why didn't I hear it?" "You tell me. Ginny's two boys had yanked a nest of them out of one of their bluebird houses. This one was still alive. Can you believe it? I transplanted the poor thing to that full phoebe's nest on the dark side of the house. And it's still there." *It sure is.* "They accepted it." *Accept it.* "See," she says, "everything eventually works out. Someday . . . oh dammit," she says, "the bus, time for the bus. Get going. I've got to leave for work. Run! Run! See you. See you, tonight. Love you." The kids and I scramble across two backyards and they just make it to the stop. "Love you, too. Later." The bus rumbles away. Then silence. Just birdsong and . . . Ginny, one of the few mornings she stood here watching her sons off: "We want bluebirds in our bluebird houses, but all we're getting are English sparrows, those worthless things." *Something so small . . .*

The Days of Blue

Six days a week at 4:40 a.m. sharp, the town crew, two men named Harold in a green town truck, rumbled down the old sewer plant road as if there was a national emergency, crying out, "Code Big Blue, Code Big Blue," trying to reach the sewer plant before the giant blue prophylactic surfaced and disappeared. They never failed. Once reaching the plant, the Harolds stationed themselves upon the galvanized observation platform, what they liked to call the crow's nest, which oversaw the waterworks. The whole hamlet, all 273 of us, sat up and waited for their holler, "Thar she blows," then the Harolds' speculation over to which one of us Big Blue belonged. No matter who, in the end, the same conclusion: no one's that big. Those days are gone. Inevitable growth. Demands for more comprehensive, long-range improvements. We've a new sewer plant, a state-of-the-art closed system. No Blue, no Harolds, no humbled waking.

Spared

The dog, some miniature form of schnauzer, I think, came rocketing off of the front porch after me. I say *think* because *bam* it crossed that invisible fence and *pop*. No, more a *poof*—gone. A voice, the voice of a woman began calling from behind the house. Everywhere, within the hidden boundary, green leaves quickly turned and peeled from the trees. "Schnitz. Schnitzie. Schnitzel." Naming the leaves, I thought, for a few seconds myself happy, drifting, gone. The woman burst out her front door, onto the porch, down the steps and . . . "Lady," I said, "stop. That's far enough. Stay where you are," and as best as I could explained the circumstances. "It's so cold," she said, briefly sobbing into a tiny red dog jacket, then staring wistfully into the tops of her empty trees. "But you saved my life. Come here," she said, holding out the red jacket as if I should slip my arms into the sleeves. "What's your name?" I almost crossed that line.

Tired of Raking

He turned and whatever blew into his head. "Spring talks intimacy all summer, but fall is really it," he said. That's because with their clothes dropped the trees were exposed. Exposed, they looked like the veins on the back of the hand. "Your hands are in my face." He said that because there was no privacy in his tight little neighborhood, especially in the fall. All the green cover gone, neighbors' houses inched closer, so close that he lived in all of them. "And all our sad sides," he said, looking at the houses. "Hell, pile 'em on." These weren't leaves swirling around the yard, but those curled foam hospital slippers. The whole crowded walk-in hospital was on its way. As it will, the fall light dimmed as if some rheostat had been turned next to off. A young woman out cold on a Gurney and intended for post-op rolled into his yard. "Day surgery," he said. In the last light of the day, her white bedding cast a pulsing glow. He had an urge to bend down and kiss her, but knew better than that. "Lawsuit," he said. Soon she would wake disoriented and want something for the pain. He had nothing but a rake.

III. Compensatorium

There Are Loyalties
Which Can't Be Taught

Foremost, the moon's to the sun,
whose true tendency is to leave
and never come back.

Even the greatest in our world
still needs reminding of its place.
And then, far below, there is us.

The moon's secondary loyalty is to us
in our neutered world, where,
not too far away, there are pounds for moons

as there are pounds for stray dogs,
and your mother
or your father-in-law discourages the notion

of letting it sleep with you
when you bring it home,
even though they let theirs sleep with them.

"By God they didn't get theirs from any pound!"
"And don't, especially don't, let it
sleep with its head on your pillow

or breathe in your ear," they say.
Fortunately, your tendency is to let it.
Just once. Such a sweet thing.

Who could ever give it up?
Hasn't it pulled things back into their right places?
Now it sleeps like a dog—heavily—

and you reach out, wanting
just to touch, to caress, to...Nowhere close yet
and you feel jerking, spasms.

It's always being chased or chasing. Sad,
so sad. It can't be any other way.

Bundle

Lavish extras—butter, cream, jam;
the littlest encouragement to blow off the day,
stick. Finally, a tug at the skirt of your two-piece

linen suit. "Quit teasing," you said. "It's unfair.
I have to get to work." I did too. A few minutes after you left,
the buzzer rang. It was you returning, giving in. Without checking

the door, opening it, there stood an elderly woman
wearing a spazzed nylon nightgown, fuzzy pink slip-ons,
long white hair let down. Behind her, on the street, idled

a Checker Cab half swallowed in exhaust. Because at the buzzer
I saw you completely falling into my arms, and further, she was you
sixty years ahead. "Here, Dear, is what you asked for," you said,

and handed over a poorly wrapped paper bundle.
Immediately, the cabby laid on the horn. You turned,
shuffled to the cab, got in and took off,

without looking back left off
long underwear; on each label,
scribed in indelible ink, the wrong initials.

Compensatorium

My great grandfather burst out of that dark hole,
the boot room off of the back porch,
his house as it was,
clapboard, trim, shutters all tight,
all one yellow.

Hopped right into a wake
of confused white pullets,
As it is, I was one of his banded hens,
my nervous head turned all for an eye,
nothing too right, all one color.

In the crotch of his elbow,
he cradled a Macintosh, worked it,
worked that apple down
the arm into his good hand,
his good hand—

three whole fingers,
the rest lost to pushed slips
with power tools, his house—
and raised it up for offer,
a glistening ruby set in a ring.

Man, it looked good, but those stubs
were fat-headed worms, one way
worms which ate and ate and turned
bitter, one of the few things
I knew. I was a chicken.

The Rain Falling, Falling
Short of Falling on Me

I admit then, too, to a kind of drifting.
He had to show me, had to, his backyard,
how every plant thrived in Florida on so little.
The hanging orchids, on air. Or Jesus,
just any stick stuck in the soil
making it. Cuttings

from Jacksonville, cuttings from the Keys. My drifting
like Ponce de Leon, imagining out back
a Rousseau jungle, but interrupted
by my father's nervous sweating, his talk
desperate with its own preoccupations,
obsessive, all the way from the airport
past the world's largest wrecking truck, lowest prices, more
foreigners coming ashore

because he could not say how much he loved,
or hurt, how long he missed me.
Nothing was left that was not suggestive.
And as he stepped off
the patio it began to rain.
Two feet in front of him and beyond,

the vinyl and aluminum roofs rattled,
large leaves nodded, water crawled down the sides
of even pitchless things. Nonchalantly,
he reached in the wall of water
up to his elbows, and began washing his hands,
as if after cleaning fish or tuning an engine,

and he looked back
basking in the dryness, his grin saying,
Isn't life good here? Come and join me.
And maybe I might have
taken my father's hands,

gently led what remained of both of us
through that wall and into that backyard
had I not hesitated, thinking.
Had I not been his son.

Sea Roses

Dotting the peninsula, the pinks and whites coexist.
One requires the other. One is continually created
a sliver different, so that their combination makes for the tangy scent
that bowls us over. I shouldn't speak for everyone.

I'm already halfway out, among them. I'm already heady,
in odd light. I better sit, slow down, get human, there,
on that big rock, take out my pocketknife, peel an apple.
My sunglasses make visible the striations of sulfur

adrift in the air. I don't carry apples. They bruise.
Were you hungry? Further on, little sparrows fly out from beneath
the thorns, and the roses have greetings upon every face:
Greetings, whoever you are, let's go on together from here.

Here we go. In and out the birds weave what? All the way
to the end there's that scent about us.

Frog in a Boat

The boat is moving.
In the middle, in less than an inch of water,
sloshing around my feet,
swims one bright green bait frog.
If I sit right,

every move it makes is two moves,
because the boat is moving, too.
I just learned this.
I'm seated in the bow
facing back, looking at smiling Uncle Al,

who just shoved off
and jumped aboard.
Boats help us look back.
I just learned this.
My Uncle Al took his own life.

A frog in a boat.
Good for something
besides balancing out the fly and mosquito population—
if I sit right.
My uncle was smiling.

He was right there
on the stern,
smiling, waving,
at the same time
waving me off.

Apology to the Packed Deli

Sorry. I was thinking of an aunt back home, the meat case glass, I guess, like her sun porch, the place she's spent most of her life criticizing the deaf town, the place she probably was right then, lighting a Winston Long, the fourth pot of coffee on, her wayward son about to drop in, or a dead leaf drop off the philodendron trained around the plate shelves, wound around the room maybe ten times—since I last saw her—choking completely the plate collection, the paint-by-number Last Supper. I once sat there in the dark myself refusing to delve into my cooked carrots. Outside a gutted deer hung in the elm draining. My cousin came and sat with me at the polished oak table with the caked lion's claw feet—the pride of that house. He shined the surface with his sleeves, and claimed, *Someday, this will be mine.* That's when I heard the calling, and calling again of my number, but I had already drifted too far away, and wouldn't go back.

The Green Suit

If I'm already that crotchety old man who's turned his back on
    everything, then
today's the day I'm overcome. While the cicadas buzz saw their
    way out, rest and
dry next to their caramel shells, *Goddamn them* changes to
    What the

hell. My walk-in closet walks out to hand me my outdated sheeny
    green suit in
which I fly around the old block. Just once; that's all I've got left.
    I circle back,
sink into my favorite chair, put up my feet, curl up and sleep.
    There's still that

unpredictable trickster inside of me, a boy keenly tuned to the old
    man's act, who
while the man drifts in sleep, brings to his back porch a fresh lake
    trout. While the
old man flew, the boy heard the cicadas above it all, misfiring.

The boy never before fished for a reason. This fish, though, he caught
    because it's
the only other thing he knows which, like the green suit and cicada
    wings, refuses
to stay one color. Not the cicadas, but the stench of fish left out
    too long

in the heat leads the old man to his porch. Finding, unwrapping the
    fish, he forgets
to put yesterday's clothes back on, forgets grousing about the waste
    and carries
the spoiled fish to the backyard picnic table. He can't wait to splay it,

to see what it ate. Nothing. The fish died hungry, but there is
    the squirt of roe—
round, red, opulent. Like the suit, it hangs all over him and won't
    come off.

Beautiful Baby

The cascade.
Per second tons of water pounding
in the distance. At the overlook,
just a hiss. A few gulls swooping through
to remind us it's real. All this

the backdrop for a busload
of international students,
visitors from far away
standing here for the first time, saying, "Say chiz.
Almbooger," Click-ka-jjjjjj, click-ka-jjjjjj, ka-jjjjjj,

ka-jjjjjj, ka-jjjjjj . . . laughing like the gulls, laughing
at themselves trying American. My mother has gone back
to the car to get the camera.
I don't even know why
I brought up Betty—if that's her name—

some vague image of her in a strapless piece,
and the night she danced upon the gala dinner table,
and my father dove for one of the high heels she kicked off.
All that pieced together by their argument I listened to that night.
A cascade. Maybe it was these falls,

slowly unzipping, curling back,
these visitors trying on America,
lust thundering in every clear space,
gulls roving hungry, never satisfied—
myself included. And how

quickly my mother turned when I mentioned Betty,
immediately reached back—further—to the time
when I was newborn, red, swaddled in blankets
and brought here. Just to say, "One beautiful baby.
Oh, such tiny feet." Half of it. The rest? I kicked off a booty,

over the rail and it landed near the edge.
A 200-foot drop. This one.
And my father dangerously straddled that rail.
Snagged it. A crowd watching, oohing, clapping,
cameras flashing, he slipped it back on.

Considering Age and Memory Loss, Remembering My First Boat

Forget that plywood tub, the body,
that plow in the water.
Ah, but the five horse blue Evinrude
pushing it, the mind. Keeps chugging,

though parts daily drop off.
Even if I find the springs, the bolts, the . . .
forget locating the slots,
the threaded holes where they belong.

It's like this: wherever
something falls off simply fills in—
what the engine needs to do
in order to keep humming along.

Out in the middle, no land in sight,
I cut the engine, remove the cover.
Some part goes over the side.
Kerplunk. So what. The engine fires

right off. It sounds looney,
but while it keeps running like this,
keeps dropping parts, the lake fills
with parts. Someday, somewhere

out there on the lake, the engine
finally dies. No big deal. I hop out
and walk home. When it's that shallow,
who needs a boat?

My Double Comes Home

It's dusk when he arrives tanned
from the many exotic
places I've wanted to visit—
any place but here. The first
words out of his mouth: "How's *our*
yard; how's *our* kids and wife? How
are we doing?" Like the too
familiar waiter—when I'm really out—
he's made a deadly assumption,
that because he momentarily
makes me happy I like him,
he should drop by anytime
for a beer. "How's our back deck?
Did we finish yet?" Tonight
he's in too much of a hurry
to assume me, as so many times
I have him. It doesn't go
both ways. "Come around back," I say,
"I'll show you." The fireflies are out.
On then off—moving on to
another place. On again,
then . . . "We finished the deck. Why
it's huge," he says, "the size
of an international
airport. And what views. As striking
as any in the world." *Yes,
I think, we do good work. I guess
a few beers won't hurt.* The more
we pour the clearer his desire.
A big moon helps. He wants to
come home, land for good. "Here?"
I've never been clearer myself:
"No sir, I need you out there.
Now." He doesn't have the options
to ask where or whine that he
has no place to go. It's the first

it's crossed my mind that he too
might be dissatisfied, the first
time I've felt him swing and miss.

On the Wing

... 39,000 feet." Really? Don't see them,
imagine, though, all the pitter patter
given the ice chatter in my plastic glass.
Which is it, plastic or glass? Sure do get small
in a hurry. All this silliness, diversion from fear
of going down. Yup, I see it, beneath me,
the sun breaking up. You're right, vacation,
let it go. If it really happened, I'd never know.
Let God. Those cumulus clouds—let them serve
as brains. One sunny side up on the brain—
some pan-o-rama. God served through glory holes
in the head. I should never sit on the wing. It moves
too much; it's man made. Next year,
we'll do it differently, plan ahead. Plan a head?
Holy idea. You'll do the packing.

Day Lilies

Sometimes it's not wind-related—
their nodding. It's to do with a multitude

of nearly indecipherable messages,
then each nod a single understanding,

their velvet ears trained
to a world's troubles blown in. Whose?

Which ones? They can't say.
They just spread so fast, don't they? Outlast

our oldest ruins; hold the original outline.
But what if the wind dies?

They keep nodding.
It's harder to see, more subtle.

They're really not listening.
These are the polite nods,

while something else is ticking,
something better going on upstairs.

An Improvement Over the Rocks

Our town has its quiet green
New England common,
around that center the shuttered green
and white Capes in a row.

Across the pinched harbor bay,
out on the stretched neck
curling the other way,
there are all the converted cottages,

varieties of colors together and alone,
once slapped and held together (by what?)
for summer, converted now to year round.
No one truly summers anymore—too much

lingering. To travel from old to new
or new to old—it cannot be avoided—
there's the town's present attraction,
the temporary bridge, erected

while the original is repaired,
or that's what residents on the green claim,
while those settling in the cottages
are sure the old one's coming down

completely, that temporary
is not temporary at all, but new.
It always depends where you live.
Can you see it—the two bridges

connecting the same two pieces of land,
one left quiet, the other getting all
the traffic? Presently, the forgotten bridge,
the one coming down or under repair,

best pleases a swarm of gulls,
who find that shellfish dropped
to the macadam never slip back
into the sea, an improvement over the rocks.

The poor shellfish,
and those few who stay home
and go nowhere and get to watch.
Nudged up alongside the whichever

way you see it bridge
are two old rusty barges
with hoisting cranes dangling their generators
like charms on someone's bracelet.

We all love our children
no matter what, that's the one
consolation. Work has yet to begin—
on both barges a lot of steel beams

either going up or coming down.
Out early on the temporary or new bridge
this morning there's the steady town
drunk looking rather shocked, clutching

the bright rail. He's staring across
at the other bridge. How could it
be over there if he's standing on it?
Leave it to the drunk.

Arson & Prophets

The hottest summer evenings a fire
rages through a nearby abandoned tinder box tenement—
flaring, shooting straight up into the night sky.

Over time a consumed man, assumed homeless, begins to show
on the day after the fires. While what remains still smolders,
he gives the fire a prophet's name. There's Jesus.

"Jesus roared, was so fast," he says. "No one had a chance."
The next night's fire is Mohammed.
"Mohammed was intolerant, brutal," the man proclaims

to the cordoned off ruins, himself reeling in the yellow tape.
Buddha is the third fire. "With Buddha," he begins, but
the many gathered neighbors talking—"our terror,

our emotional loss because we live in fear; our
drop in property values; our . . . ."—
makes it impossible to hear his claim.

Late that night there's the sound of firemen shattering windows,
their urgent voices shouting, "Hurry up, hurry up."
Not for more hoses and water, but calling

in case that poor man sleeps inside. When they wake,
there is no fire.

The House That Goldilocks Built

She's nothing like the book said—
someone else's story, someone else's
bad day. Maybe you totally identify.

That's why this poem walked in
on your life. All the more reason
you soundly agree with what it tells you:

thus wronged she had the right
to vanish; therapeutic that thick in the deep forest
she fell into then took advantage of

a sunken foundation, piece by hewn piece
built out of it, over it,
very much in the tradition of all tales.

Today she has herself a cozy cottage,
years lived in isolation, one story filled
with the fewest possible things

to worry about or go wrong—
a roof, a floor, a fire. You show up
at her door. She blankly invites you in,

throws you down and sits on you.
Good for you, good for Goldilocks—
you didn't break.

At 18 or 19

All day stooped in that boiling vineyard,
tying the heads of limp tendrils with a slip knot
of baling twine—delicate work, a lot of time
the heads slipping out. Eventually, though,
leading them up, securing them to the first wire
where they did the rest, their weaving.
I hated the work, but I said, "It's good work."
I didn't know what it meant yet,
that the limp heads kept slipping out,
but it related to splitting a grape,
how the pulp closest to the surface tasted sweet,
while the rest was just this big glob of nothing
which you gulped or spat out. One thing
I could say with certainty: the vineyard,
with its strung wires, was a kind of loom.
Not exactly original.
There was an early Industrial Age loom
which I'd seen in the vineyard owner's house.
A retired historian and Thoreau scholar,
he worshipped that loom in his large front room.
"He doesn't know what to do with it.
Just taking up space. One strange companion."
That's what I said. In a lot of ways I knew
I was talking about myself, but it was too late,
I'd already said it, jumped into the passenger seat
of the yellow Impala convertible
owned by a flush, shiny-faced man named John,
a bartender I just met, who all month ventured out,
parked his car beside the tool shed,
which offered the best view of the vineyard. There
he began his day as mine ended. Don't ask me why.
Strange? Yes, everything was strange to us,
that was a premium, that's why we met,
that's what we liked about each other.
John never put the convertible top down,
and that too had something to do with the skin

of a grape, or us. "Oh cut that shit out.
Stop hogging the joint." We said that to one another
a lot. And "Ooh, this landscape—everywhere, baby,
it's so beautiful here." Our view swept all the way
to the far end of the vineyard,
the sparse, dirt-brown end where I'd been working,

where the new vineyard would fail to take hold,
but for the moment I saw it already unfurling.
Filling in, that someday I'd return at harvest
to say, "I planted those grapes."

The Widow's Drought Dream

Her drowned, never found husband came flailing through
the swamp's brittle hedge, swimming almost. He swore

this time he left the wagon tied up on the other side
of the flood-cresting fork, with it that easily spooked mare

that took his life. "Hold on, hold on," he cried, hard to tell who
he addressed, not where he was. Slimy weeds trailed his arms

and legs. A long branch of choke hid his face. "What a mess," he said,
yanked taut a wisp and cleanly cut it above the crotch. She now knew

his intentions, had seen her father fix a dowsing stick when ten.
"Now this," he said, taking hold of the stick's reins, "is the only horse

a man should trust," and like that drove her meager stamp of land.
When the stick took off for water, he jammed his heel into the dirt

as if braking, set his dig mark just short of the front gate.
"How deep is it?" is all she asked. Struggling in her shriveled jonquils,

he repeated, "Make it home, make it home, make it home."

Love Poem with Balls

"It's about you. It's always about you, isn't it?"
my kid-laden wife said, this ending about the same complaint,
me leaving the house to play a Sunday pick-up game.
"No," I said, "specifically, if you really care, this is about bocce,
this special leather traveling case under my arm full of bocce balls,
their relationship to the planets, the tiny red planet the gods throw
out first, winners decided by who glows furthest from hottest.

"It does too make sense. Balls—with their games—beg attention
to metaphor, both good in any dispute—even political or diplomatic—
and the world is a better place given both." "No," she said, "a ball
is a politician, a metaphor is a diplomat, all one step up from a rock,
and I'd like to throw you for the distance." "That's it! That's the feel
of it," I said, "the ball's demand on the hand along with the mold
of the mind, to question, 'What can this baby do?' But it's not that

so much as what balls do to us—as with this argument—
their progression, their history from solid and more malicious
to air-filled, less projectile, more bounce. How, for instance,
I've been lobbing the kids' soccer ball at grey squirrels up in the
    oak tops
because they pillage all the starch out of the acorns, when really
    they float
tiny French berets on our heads, beautiful, small Parisian disruptions
in the fall. Or how last night's croquet balls pleasantly clacked
    when struck

after *I'm going to send you*—yes, I'm talking about us—and how
the fragile glass marbles ticking in my palm were—minutes ago—
boulders flushed through the mountain pass after a torrential
    downpour.
Yes, it sounds immortal. Sure, it can stop there."

Morning Is Best

With her, the barn's attached to the house.
The thin wall between us steams. All night,
animal stirring, heaves, isolated fits or coughs.
Morning is best. The chickens, dogs, goats
and pigs in the kitchen are flush, embarrassed.
And when we burn it down, nothing's excluded.
The villagers get what they want,
more than they think—odder combinations
mate without a care. Every thing loses specificity,
that which it's designed to do, yet without nerves,
twitches; without muscle, arches; without a mouth,
whines; without a heart, bleeds. What's left?
Only the foundation spiked with saplings,
the bed of nails, pieces of melted windows—knotted,
seized, brain-like—complete strangers shuffling through.

Two Old Horses

There we are in the field.
A morning star winks above.
The moon is missing.
The grass lies down
like the tufts of course hair over their eyes.
Eyes in the grass. No place to stir
that isn't obvious. Hold on.
They nip and pull each other's brows,
and chew. The jaws work
given the smallest piece of you—not just up
and down, but at the same time sliding
sideways. The sun comes up; the world turns,
but charts a diagonal streak instead of an aura.
Double scissors action. Double back pleasure:
wine on the label of last night's empty bottle
here pronounced *win - eee*. They'd like to
crawl up in one another's mouth, but they're full.
Look at their sunken spines, their sagging bellies.
Last night they finished off the moon.